Activities for
FAST FINISHERS
Math

By Marc Tyler Nobleman

SCHOLASTIC
PROFESSIONAL BOOKS

NEW YORK • TORONTO • LONDON • AUCKLAND • SYDNEY
MEXICO CITY • NEW DELHI • HONG KONG • BUENOS AIRES

Cover design by Maria Lilja
Cover art by Jeff Shelly
Interior design by Solutions by Design, Inc.
Interior illustration by Mike Moran

ISBN: 0-439-35532-X

CONTENTS

ABOUT THIS BOOK

It happens to teachers all the time. A class is taking a test or working on a project and a few students finish sooner than the rest. They're sitting around, looking bored. What can you give them so they'll use what's left of the time period in a valuable and enriching way?

That's where this book can be of help. It's full of high-interest math activities that your students are sure to love. Does your class like crossword puzzles? Then they'll love the number puzzles in these pages. Do they like to figure out and break codes? Inside, they'll have plenty of opportunities to solve a host of number-related mysteries.

In this book, "math puzzle" does not mean "math problem." Each puzzle or game is a refreshing and fun challenge that reinforces the math curriculum while building other valuable skills, such as creative thinking or visual perception. There are 55 one-page activities in all, designed to be worked on independently and keep those fast finishers busy for an average of 10 to 15 minutes each. The checklist on the next page will help you and your students keep track of their progress.

This book has been designed to entertain your students while slipping in some education at the same time. It aims to help students learn that math can be both useful and enjoyable.

—*Marc Tyler Nobleman*

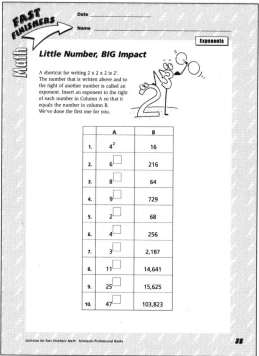

Student Checklist

Math

Track Your Progress Form

Put a ✔ in the box for each activity you complete.

Date _____

Name _____

Time for the Future

A time capsule is a box filled with items from a certain period of time and buried for people in the future to dig up. A time mathsule is very similar, except you need to use math to know when it was buried. When was each time mathsule buried? Add up the numbers that are part of each mathsule. The total is the year it was buried. (There is a lot of stuff in each—these are very big time mathsules!)

1. 900 Confederate coins
   82 hats
   439 newspapers
   445 arrowheads

   Total _____

   _____

2. 314 essays by schoolchildren
   60 train tickets
   740 food labels
   567 "I Went to the Moon" buttons
   288 expired drivers' licenses

   Total _____

   _____

3. 500 postage stamps
   202 compact discs
   set of 24 encyclopedias
   582 adhesive bandages
   90 pounds of instant oatmeal
   592 bottle caps

   Total _____

4. passports from 79 countries
   435 menus
   copies of 773 birth announcements
   168 fishing hooks
   100 crayons
   lyrics to 50 popular songs
   phone books from 342 cities

   Total _____

   _____

5. 23 dog collars
   13 magazines
   signatures of 38 mayors
   26 flags
   1801 newspapers

   Total _____

   _____

6. $200 cash
   320 wooden spoons
   681 broken watches
   596 photographs
   102 bow ties

   Total _____

YOUR TURN

Create a mathsule from the year 476.

Math

Many Pennies Lane

The Beatles were one of the most famous rock bands of the 20th century. One of their most well-known songs was called "Penny Lane." Look at the list of song titles below. How would they be renamed when converted to pennies? You may write with numbers instead of writing out your answer in words. The first one is done for you.

Song title	Song title converted to pennies
1. "Twenty Dollars Lane"	"2,000 Pennies Lane"
2. "Seven Dollars Lane"	
3. "Sixty-One Quarters Lane"	
4. "One Hundred Eleven Nickels Lane"	
5. "Two Dollars and Nineteen Cents Lane"	
6. "Four Hundred Dimes Lane"	
7. "Eighty-One Dollars and One Cent Lane"	
8. "One Dollar and Ninety-Nine Cents Lane"	
9. "Penny and Dollar Lane"	
10. "Ninety-One Half-Dollars Lane"	
11. "Three Dollars and Twenty Nickels Lane"	
12. "One Thousand Dollars Lane"	

Date _____

Name _____

Math

Half Time

Each equation has one number that, when removed, creates a new equation with a sum that is exactly half of the original. Find that number and circle it. Write the new equation on the line beneath the original. There is only one correct answer for each. We've done the first one for you.

1. (23) + 16 + 7 = 46

   16 + 7 = 23 (which is half of 46)

2. 15 + 7 + 12 + 34 = 68

   _____

3. 11 + 3 + 6 + 2 = 22

   _____

4. 21 + 38 + 67 + 8 = 134

   _____

5. 61 + 94 + 33 = 188

   _____

6. 24 + 30 + 100 + 180 + 26 = 360

   _____

7. 77 + 368 + 46 + 245 = 736

   _____

8. 610 + 401 + 102 + 107 = 1,220

   _____

9. 239 + 812 + 1,329 + 278 = 2,658

   _____

10. 1,035 + 1,507 + 5,421 + 2,879 = 10,842

    _____

YOUR TURN

Did you find a strategy that helped you figure out which number to remove? Describe it here.

Grab, Add 'N Win!

Ten lucky radio station listeners were chosen to
participate in this year's 101.3 FM's annual Grab 'N
Add shopping spree. They had 101.3 seconds to grab
as much as they could. However, only the participant
whose item prices added up closest to—but not more
than—$101.30 got to keep it all. Who was that? Do
the math and write your answers on the blanks
below. Then circle the name of the winner!

Name	Items and prices	Total value
1. Deena	$40 blouse, $10 book, $30 pair of sunglasses	
2. Noelle	$15 board game, $42.50 software, $12 earrings, $31 scarf	
3. Gerry	$28.99 basketball, $72.89 sneakers	
4. Raphael	$1.75 picture frame, $14 video, $3.50 magazine, $81 camera	
5. Francesca	$51 jacket, $22.30 bookends, $25.68 gumball machine, $2.33 bag of gumballs	
6. Joel	$38 travel bag, $16.70 canteen, $37.50 raincoat, $9.08 compact disc	
7. Alexandra	$29.99 heart-shaped waffle iron, $15.75 heart-shaped picture frame, $20 heart-shaped box of chocolates, $24 heart-shaped mirror	
8. Samantha	$69 pink bicycle, $29.99 bicycle helmet, $13.75 bicycle accessories	
9. Sebastian	$79.99 cell phone, $19.99 sports jersey, $1.50 candy bar	
10. Anthony	$35 skateboard, $10 poster, $19.99 lava lamp	

Date _____

Name _____

Desperately Seeking 68

Look at the groups of numbers below.
Rearrange them in the correct order so that
when you subtract, the difference equals 68.
There's only one correct answer for each.
We've done the first one for you.

1. 2 1 5 4 2 ⟶ <u>122 – 54 = 68</u>

2. 7 9 7 ⟶ _____

3. 9 5 3 2 ⟶ _____

4. 3 1 0 1 3 ⟶ _____

5. 6 6 8 3 1 ⟶ _____

6. 2 1 0 5 8 ⟶ _____

7. 0 1 2 0 1 7 ⟶ _____

8. 9 7 2 3 5 3 ⟶ _____

9. 1 2 3 5 5 9 ⟶ _____

10. 6 7 9 6 7 9 ⟶ _____

YOUR TURN

Create your own number mix that can be rearranged to form a subtraction
equation that equals 86.

Numberless Subtraction

When you think of the word *unicycle*, do you think of the number one? Many people don't, even though the word contains the prefix *uni-*, which means one. Below, you'll find several words, phrases, or places associated with a number. Figure out the number for each, then subtract and find the difference. You may use reference books if you need help. We've done the first one for you.

1. Tripod – unicorn = __3 – 1 = 2_____

2. Quintuplets – quartet = _____

3. Valentine's Day – Groundhog Day = _____

4. Octagon – pentagon = _____

5. Planets in our solar system – continents = _____

6. U.S. senators – U.S. states = _____

7. Minutes in an hour – days in September = _____

8. Year the Declaration of Independence was signed – year Columbus first landed in the Americas = _____

9. Millennium year – the year exactly one century before the millennium = _____

10. Tetrahedron – quadrant = _____

YOUR TURN

Create a numberless subtraction equation like the ones above.

FAST FINISHERS

Math

Big Spenders

Who's the biggest spender in the group of people listed below? You'll need to subtract some money to find out. Write how much money each person had left over after making purchases at the drugstore. Then rank each spender according to who was richest before (#1) to who's richest now (#8).

Purchase Price:

book — $5.99	vitamins — $8.25
laundry detergent — $7.50	notebook — $0.99
box of pens — $1	cotton balls — $1.99
toothbrush — $2.49	garbage bags — $4.59

Name	Total money	Items purchased	Money left over	Rank
1. Juan	$14	book, cotton balls		
2. Kevin	$17	box of pens, garbage bags		
3. Mike	$18.59	book, toothbrush, vitamins		
4. Dara	$8.75	cotton balls, toothbrush		
5. Randi	$12.13	notebook, box of pens		
6. Seth	$21.80	laundry detergent (2), cotton balls		
7. Darren	$40.06	garbage bags, vitamins (3)		
8. Raquel	$23	book (2), box of pens (2), vitamins		

A Perfect Match

Each number in column 1 is separated by exactly 343 from a number in column 2. It is either 343 more than or 343 less than a column 2 number. Add or subtract to find out the pairs that are 343 apart. Then draw a line from one column to the other linking the pairs together.

Column 1	Column 2
656	818
251	594
854	456
799	914
686	1,226
475	999
976	343
466	511
1,257	123
883	633

Eight Is Great

It's the year 2000, and eight-year-old Stephanie is celebrating her birthday on the same day her family is having a reunion. To celebrate Stephanie's birthday, instead of name badges, everyone is wearing the number of years before Stephanie they were born. Use those numbers to answer the questions in the chart below and figure out what year each of these family members was (or will be) eight years old.

Hi, I'm 5

Stephanie's...	Badge says	Year born	Year turned eight
1. father	29		
2. mother	28		
3. great-grandfather	79		
4. great-grandmother	77		
5. grandmother	55		
6. grandfather	54		
7. aunt	23		
8. uncle	27		
9. brother	5		
10. dog (in human years!)	1		
11.			

YOUR TURN

How many years before Stephanie were you born? Add your information to the bottom of the chart in the space provided.

Date _____

Name _____

Radio Riches

Several local radio stations are running wild promotions with cash prizes. Want to take part? First, figure out how much each station's award is when calculated on a daily basis. Use division to calculate each offer and write your answers in the last column of the chart. We've done the first one for you.

Radio station	Money offered	If listener does what	For how long	Amount of money when calculated daily
1. WDEA	$1,000	lives in tree house	2 weeks	$1000 ÷ 14 = $71.43
2. WSMK	$500	doesn't talk	1 day	
3. WMLC	$5,000	wears earmuffs everywhere	30 days	
4. WAJD	$2,500	hands out radio station bumper stickers	1 week	
5. WMRP	$1,500	tutors children after school	3 weeks	
6. WWFD	$10,000	cleans litter off local streets	25 days	
7. WPET	$750	finds homes for stray dogs and cats	3 days	
8. WWHY	$25,000	trains and runs in the marathon to promote station's fitness campaign	75 days	
9. WHIP	$3,000	writes catchy new slogan for station	5 days	
10. WZZZ	$7,500	gets the most donations from people in support of station fundraiser	7 days	

Which contest or contests would you want to enter and why?

_____

Date _____

Name _____

Tag Sale Tally

Every year, Sean sells some compact discs from his huge collection at his family's tag sale. Every year, he slightly raises the price for each CD. Put the tag sale prices in order from the earliest tag sale (least expensive) to most recent tag sale (most expensive). To do this, you'll need to figure out how much each CD costs in each year. There is only one correct order.

Tag sale price	Cost per CD	Rank (1=earliest, 10=most recent)
12 CDs for $6.00		
8 CDs for $6.00		
4 CDs for $8.00		
7 CDs for $7.00		
9 CDs for $2.25		
4 CDs for $6.00		
5 CDs for $9.95		
4 CDs for $10.00		
5 CDs for $14.95		
5 CDs for $4.95		

Date _____

Name _____

Good Things Come in Threes

Three of the four numbers in each series below can be used to create four equations that are true. Rearrange the three numbers to find one true equation. Then, thanks to inverse operations, you will always be able to find three more equations that are true. We've done the first one for you.

Numbers	Equations
1. 28, 4, 12, 7	$28 \div 7 = 4$, $28 \div 4 = 7$, $4 \times 7 = 28$, and $7 \times 4 = 28$
2. 4, 6, 3, 7	_____
3. 38, 26, 2, 19	_____
4. 9, 36, 3, 4	_____
5. 17, 13, 5, 12	_____
6. 18, 32, 48, 50	_____
7. 56, 54, 9, 6	_____
8. 76, 6, 19, 4	_____
9. 20, 2, 25, 5	_____
10. 6, 42, 7, 49	_____

YOUR TURN

Put together a sequence of four numbers like the ones above and see if your classmates can figure out the three numbers that form a true equation.

Date _____

Name _____

Number Pole

You've probably seen lots of barber poles, but have you ever seen a number pole? To complete the number pole below, you'll need to solve each equation by adding, subtracting, multiplying, or dividing. How do you know which operation to choose? Find the solution that yields a number that helps the center of the number pole go from 1 at the top to 9 at the bottom. An answer can have either two or three digits. There is only one correct answer for each. We've done the first one for you.

Number pole

1. 17 $\underline{+}$ 14 =	3	1	
2. 84 ___ 7 =		2	
3. 54 ___ 16 =		3	
4. 16 ___ 4 =		4	
5. 32 ___ 8 =		5	
6. 124 ___ 42 =		6	
7. 651 ___ 273 =		7	
8. 1,440 ___ 3 =		8	
9. 377 ___ 13 =		9	

YOUR TURN

Create a number pole that starts with 12 and goes to 21. The answers to your equations can have answers with either two, three, or four digits.

Date _____

Name _____

Meanie Genie

The Meanie Genie grants three wishes, but only to students who know their math—including the correct order of operations. Anyone who gets the math correct in Genie's math challenge will receive ALL his or her wishes. Anyone who gets even one equation wrong receives NO wishes! Check each person's math, and circle yes or no to show which students' wishes will be granted. We've done the first one for you.

TIP *Order of operations is important. Do multiplication first, then division, next addition, and finally subtraction!*

1. Darrel

Genie's challenge	Equals	Darrel's wishes: YES or NO?
45 – 36 – 8 =	1	new bike
3 x 16 ÷ 6 ÷ 4 =	2	world peace
19 – 10 + 3 =	12	sunshine every day

Meanie Genie explains: _Darrel gets no wishes granted because he got one wrong! (The third equation should equal 6.)_

2. Jake

Genie's challenge	Equals	Jake's wishes: YES or NO?
65 ÷ 13 – 4 =	1	catch a ball in a baseball stadium
8 x 3 ÷ 12 =	2	tacos for lunch every day
6 + 5 + 3 – 11 =	3	go inside a space shuttle

Meanie Genie explains: _____

_____

3. Cecilia

Genie's challenge	Equals	Cecilia's wishes: YES or NO?
1 x 1 x 0 =	0	new dress
4 ÷ 4 + 0 + 1 =	2	no puppies without homes
30 – 10 ÷ 2 =	5	ice cream shop opens on her street

Meanie Genie explains: _____

_____

4. Daniela

Genie's challenge	Equals	Daniela's wishes: YES or NO?
36 ÷ 4 + 1 – 9 =	1	visit a movie set
100 ÷ 5 x 2 – 8 =	2	see her name in the newspaper
3 + 4 + 8 ÷ 2 =	11	new car for her parents

Meanie Genie explains: _____

_____

Date _____

Name _____

Fraction Word Problems

Get the Scoop!

It's the annual ice cream scooping contest where people compete to see who can stack the most scoops of ice cream. Last year's winner, Darby, had 24 scoops! How did this year's participants do? Use the clues to find out. Then write the winner's name in the blank below.

Participants	Clues	Number of scoops
1. Zaura	one scoop chocolate chip, two caramel swirl, four raspberry	
2. Ellis	twelve scoops cookie dough, half as many mint chocolate chip	
3. Clara	six scoops banana, twice as many fudge swirl	
4. Darby	three scoops vanilla, four times as many chocolate	
5. Chang	five scoops strawberry, half as many raspberry as Zaura	
6. Thelma	20 scoops rocky road, one-fourth as many butter pecan, and one-fifth as many cookies and cream as butter pecan	
7. Deon	half as many banana as Clara, one-third mint chocolate chip as banana, and ten times caramel swirl as mint chocolate chip	
8. Gabriela	twelve scoops vanilla, two-thirds that amount of cinnamon stick, and three times as many super fudge chunk as cinnamon stick	

This year's super scooper is _____!

Activities for Fast Finishers: Math Scholastic Professional Books

Date _____

Name _____

Whole Number Computation

The Number Shuffle

Below are two really "cool" fun fact riddles. In order to find the answer you'll need to shuffle some numbers. Write the solution to each equation in the blank and also in the *first* blank of the *next* equation. The solution of the last equation will give you the riddle answer! We've done the first one for you.

How many square miles is America's largest city, Juneau, Alaska?

1. 36 + _**390**_ = 426

2. _____ + 876 = _____

3. 486 + _____ = _____

4. _____ − 654 = _____

5. _____ x 3 = _____

6. 6,402 − _____ = _____

Riddle answer:

America's largest city is _____ square miles.

How many degrees below zero does it sometimes get in the coldest place in the United States?

7. 59 + _____ = 209

8. _____ − 79 = _____

9. 639 + _____ = _____

10. _____ − 560 = _____

11. _____ ÷ 30 = _____

12. 85 − _____ = _____

Riddle answer:

The temperature can drop to _____ degrees below zero in Alaska.

Date _____

Name _____

A-Maze-ing!

To run through this maze, you'll need to add, subtract, multiply, and divide. To get from start to finish, shade only the boxes where the number can equal exactly 18 using the suggested operation. Positive numbers only please!

Examples:

5 x	→ don't shade: no number can be multiplied by 5 to evenly equal 18
6 x	→ shade: 6 x 3 = 18
11 +	→ shade: 11 + 7 = 18
31 +	→ don't shade: no number can be added to 31 to equal 18

START					
18 +	54 ÷	32 ÷	36 +	48 ÷	98 ÷
42 ÷	9 x	20 +	12 x	54 +	9 –
19÷	4 +	19 +	15 –	4 x	22 ÷
25 +	108 ÷	21 –	38 ÷	16 –	96 ÷
15 –	0 x	18 –	36 ÷	36 –	100 +
3 –	26 ÷	78 ÷	8 x	2 x	14 x
7 x	28 +	24 +	56 ÷	199 –	17 –
64 ÷	92 ÷	12 –	44 ÷	18 x	702 ÷
10 x	36 x	30 +	11 x	146 ÷	3 x
					FINISH

YOUR TURN

Create a maze in which a friend or family member must find his or her way through by shading every operation that can be completed to equal 30.

Date _____

Name _____

Lights, Camera, Action!

You're the assistant producer for the popular game show "Who Wants to Win Ten Dollars?" On the show, contestants have ten seconds to solve an equation. Then they must guess which of four doors the correct answer is hidden behind. Winning requires skill and luck. The show's producer has just given you the equations for tomorrow's show, each accompanied by four possible answers (one for each door). Solve each equation and circle the correct answer so the producer will know when to give out the prize money.

Welcome to
"Who Wants
to Win
Ten Dollars?"

Equation	**Producer's possible answers**			
1. 56 + 46 =	100	101	102	106
2. 62 − 26 =	63	36	26	16
3. 48 x 4 =	129	188	208	192
4. 340 ÷ 68 =	5	6	18	4
5. 23 + 59 =	80	82	83	85
6. 6 x 33 =	199	145	198	186
7. 656 ÷ 8 =	80	82	83	85
8. 562 − 268 =	294	298	268	283
9. 76 x 76 =	5,243	5,657	5,776	6,557
10. 1,446 + 327 =	1,772	1,773	1,779	1,777
11. 133 x 25 =	3,333	3,395	3,325	3,345
12. 1,482 ÷ 13 =	116	118	113	114

YOUR TURN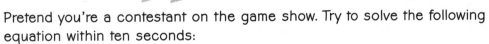

Pretend you're a contestant on the game show. Try to solve the following equation within ten seconds:

689 ÷ 13 = _____.

Date _____

Name _____

Math

Reaching the Top

It takes more than climbing skills to reach the top of these ladders! Our climbers need to know how to do math. In order to climb to the next rung, each equation must be correct. Check our climbers' math to see who climbed the highest.

1.

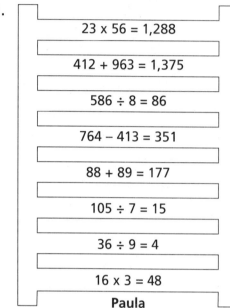

23 x 56 = 1,288

412 + 963 = 1,375

586 ÷ 8 = 86

764 − 413 = 351

88 + 89 = 177

105 ÷ 7 = 15

36 ÷ 9 = 4

16 x 3 = 48

Paula

3.

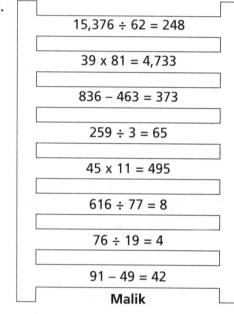

15,376 ÷ 62 = 248

39 x 81 = 4,733

836 − 463 = 373

259 ÷ 3 = 65

45 x 11 = 495

616 ÷ 77 = 8

76 ÷ 19 = 4

91 − 49 = 42

Malik

2.

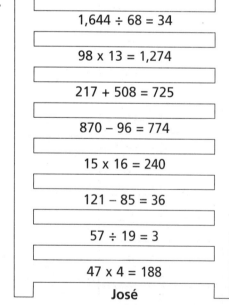

1,644 ÷ 68 = 34

98 x 13 = 1,274

217 + 508 = 725

870 − 96 = 774

15 x 16 = 240

121 − 85 = 36

57 ÷ 19 = 3

47 x 4 = 188

José

4.

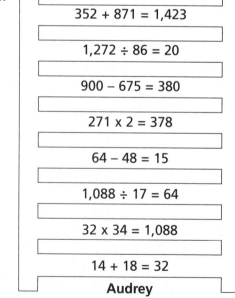

352 + 871 = 1,423

1,272 ÷ 86 = 20

900 − 675 = 380

271 x 2 = 378

64 − 48 = 15

1,088 ÷ 17 = 64

32 x 34 = 1,088

14 + 18 = 32

Audrey

Who climbed the highest? _____

Date _____

Name _____

Harvest Riddle

For each pair of numbers, separately complete
four operations: addition, subtraction, multiplication,
and division. (Always subtract the smaller from the
larger, and always divide the smaller into the larger.)

EXAMPLE: 45, 5

Addition:	45 + 5 = 50
Subtraction:	45 − 5 = 40
Multiplication:	45 x 5 = 225
Division:	5 ÷ 5 = 9

Shade all results in the grid. When you're done, hold this page at arm's length
from your face, and you'll see the answer to this riddle:

How many legs does a harvestman have? _____

1. 64, 8 _____

2. 18, 3 _____

3. 35, 7 _____

4. 6, 0 _____

60	9	258	130	1
12	56	15	512	182
19	54	79	6	14
25	5	28	72	76
168	8	44	245	954
201	42	0	21	26
55	87	4	34	51

Math

Three's a Charm

Within each series of numbers below are three numbers that are the same number apart from one another. To find the three numbers, you'll need to decide what was added to each number to get to the next number. Once you've identified the evenly spaced trio in each series, write the three numbers in the chart. Also, tell how many apart each trio member is from the next. We've done the first one for you.

Number series	Evenly spaced trio	How many apart from one another?
1. 3, 19, 22, 28, 41, 44	3, 22, 41	19
2. 26, 29, 36, 39, 40, 43		
3. 14, 18, 25, 30, 34, 50		
4. 11, 30, 46, 81, 87, 103		
5. 48, 63, 116, 142, 221, 298		
6. 23, 37, 49, 58, 65, 79		
7. 13, 19, 27, 64, 87, 115		
8. 1,356; 2,218; 2,323; 2,376; 2,428; 3,244		

YOUR TURN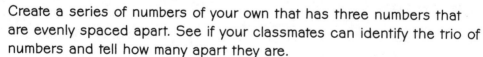

Create a series of numbers of your own that has three numbers that are evenly spaced apart. See if your classmates can identify the trio of numbers and tell how many apart they are.

Activities for Fast Finishers: Math Scholastic Professional Books

Math

Find the Bookend

Each number pattern on the list below is followed by a second list of numbers. One number from the second list fits at either the beginning or the end of the sequence, like a bookend! Figure out the number pattern. Then fill in the chart below by answering the questions. We've done one for you.

Number patterns	List	Which number belongs?	Beginning or end?	Description of pattern
1. 4, 6, 8, 10	3, 9, 12	12	end	numbers increase by 2
2. 5, 10, 15	0, 1, 5, 25			
3. 8, 13, 18, 23	3, 5, 15, 33			
4. 12, 14, 20, 22, 28, 30	4, 10, 32, 36			
5. 43, 39, 35, 31	46, 44, 27, 25			
6. 116, 109, 102	125, 123, 119, 94			
7. 2, 4, 3, 5, 4, 6, 5	8, 9, 7, 10			
8. 77, 76, 84, 83, 91, 90, 98, 97	67, 70, 98, 105			
9. 0, 3, 7, 12, 18, 25	31, 32, 33, 34			
10. 800, 400, 200, 100	75, 50, 25, 60			

YOUR TURN

Create a number pattern of your own. See if your classmates, friends, or family can figure out the pattern and the correct missing number.

Abracadabra!

Paula just started classes at a school for magicians where the first thing they test is the power of observation— an important ability for all magicians-to-be! What kind of magician would you make? See how quickly you can figure out what rule three of the four sets of numbers in each group follow. Then cross out the set of numbers that does not follow that rule. Use the space provided to explain the rule. The faster you figure it out, the sooner you'll be awarded your magic wand!

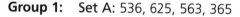

Group 1:   **Set A:** 536, 625, 563, 365

             Set B: 3,241; 1,423; 4,132; 3,441

             Set C: 4,596; 4,598; 8,945; 9,584

             Set D: 67,302; 70,326; 28,076; 27,360

             Rule: _____

             _____

Group 2:   **Set A:** 21, 54, 89, 76

             Set B: 876, 954, 654, 321

             Set C: 2,310; 5,432; 8,765; 4,321

             Set D: 65,432; 98,765; 56,432; 87,654

             Rule: _____

             _____

Group 3:   **Set A:** 214, 326, 498, 170

             Set B: 336, 438, 781, 264

             Set C: 848, 418, 274, 172

             Set D: 201, 204, 316, 458

             Rule: _____

             _____

YOUR TURN

Create your own "abracadabra" problem for a friend to solve.

Date _____

Name _____

Pyramid Challenge

Each "pyramid" below is missing some "bricks." To plug the holes, you'll need to figure out the number pattern in each pyramid's sequence of numbers. Start at the top and read left to right, writing in the missing numbers that complete each sequence on the correct bricks. Describe the pattern on the lines provided.

1.

```
            | 4  |
       | 9  | 14 | 19 |
  | 24 | 29 |    | 39 | 44 |
| 49 |    | 59 | 64 | 69 | 74 |
```

_____
_____
_____

2.

```
       |    |
  | 7  | 9  | 16 |
| 18 | 25 | 27 |    | 36 |
| 43 |    | 52 | 54 | 61 | 63 |
```

_____
_____
_____

3.

```
       | 88 |
       | 82 | 79 |
  | 76 | 73 |    | 67 | 64 |
|    | 58 |    | 52 |    | 46 | 43 |
```

_____
_____
_____

4.

```
       | 31 |
  | 30 |    | 35 |
| 41 | 40 |    | 45 | 51 |
| 50 |    | 55 |    | 60 | 66 |
```

_____
_____
_____

YOUR TURN

Try this bonus challenge and see if you can figure out the number pattern. (Hint: It doesn't involve addition or subtraction.)

```
          | 12 |
     | 3  | 24 | 6  |
| 48 | 12 |    | 24 | 192 |
|    | 384| 96 |    | 192 |1536|
```

_____
_____

FAST FINISHERS

Date _____

Name _____

Math

Think Ahead

Having a crystal ball won't help you complete this chart, but understanding number patterns will. For each number on the left, find the next highest number in which:

A) every digit is the same
(examples: 99; 222; 4,444)

B) the digits are consecutively greater by 1
(examples: 67; 345; 5,678)

The first one is done for you.

Number	A	B
1. 12	22	23
2. 78		
3. 156		
4. 333		
5. 669		
6. 1,108		
7. 2,247		
8. 5,566		
9. 7,901		
10. 9,999		

YOUR TURN

Make your own number pattern chart for a friend to complete.

Division

Hit the Road

If one digit in each number listed below "hits the road" (is removed), the remaining number will be evenly divisible by 9. Circle the number you would remove and write the new number. Then check your work by dividing the new number by 9. We've done the first one for you.

Original number	New number	Check your division here.
1. 8④1 =	81	81 ÷ 9 = 9
2. 127		
3. 263		
4. 1,395		
5. 1,880		
6. 3,206		
7. 5,385		
8. 20,151		
9. 28,531		
10. 94,122		

YOUR TURN

Can you figure out a pattern among the digits in the numbers that are evenly divisible by nine? Explain the pattern here.

_____

_____

Date _____

Name _____

Sum Good Facts

How good are you at trivia? The following questions will test your math skills while adding facts about space, science, and American History to your trivia bank. Do the math and you'll find the answer to each question.

Trivia question	Answer
1. How many humans had walked on the moon by 1972? → Add the numbers from this list that divide evenly into 16 to get the answer: 10, 5, 4, 8.	
2. Arizona was which number state admitted to the Union? → Add the numbers from this list that are evenly divisible by 6 to get the answer: 44, 12, 20, 36.	
3. On December 17, 1903, the Wright Brothers flew the world's first engine plane several times. How many seconds did the longest flight of the day last? → Add the number from this list that is evenly divisible by 4 to the one that is evenly divisible by 9 to get the answer: 27, 10, 42, 32.	
4. A whisper is 10 decibels loud. A lawn mower is 70. How many decibels is thunder? → Add all of the numbers that are evenly divisible by 3 or 7 to get the answer: 63, 27, 34, 46.	
5. "The Star-Spangled Banner" was written in 1814. How many years later did it become the national anthem? → Add the numbers from this list that are evenly divisible by 9 to get the answer: 64, 49, 45, 72.	
6. A bicentennial celebrates a 200-year anniversary. How many years does a sesquicentennial celebrate? → Add all of the answers from the right column of the chart that are evenly divisible by 6 to get the answer.	

YOUR TURN ⚡⚡

Research your own fun fact that involves a number, then create a puzzler for it like the ones above to try out on a classmate or family member.

STRENGTH in Numbers

Everyone knows there are 26 letters in the alphabet. Letter a is the first, b is the second, c is the third, and so on. Below are several statements concerning numbers. Write whether each statement is true or false by changing each letter of each word to their number equivalent in the alphabet and adding them together. We've done the first one for you.

Greater than or less than?	Do the math	True or false?
1. six > zero	s i x z e r o 19 + 9 + 24 > 26 + 5 + 18 + 15 (52 > 64)	false
2. nine > seven		
3. two > one		
4. twelve > eight		
5. eighty > sixty		
6. fifty > thirteen		
7. thirty-one > twenty-one		
8. seventy-four > forty-seven		

YOUR TURN

Create three "greater than" statements using the word form of numbers and ask a classmate, friend, or family member to determine if they're true or false.

Math

FAST FINISHERS

Prime Time for Prime Numbers

Prime time is a television term meaning the period between 8 P.M. and 11 P.M.—the time when the most people watch TV. Ed is doing research on television quality so he must watch a lot of TV. This is his TV-watching schedule for next week. Circle the shows that are both on a prime number channel and shown during prime time. Channels are listed in boldface after the shows.

A prime number is greater than 1 and cannot be evenly divided by any other number besides 1 and itself. For example, 11 is a prime number because any other number besides 1 and 11 cannot evenly divide it. The number 12 is not a prime number because, besides 1 and 12, it can be evenly divided by 2, 3, 4, and 6.

Time	Monday	Tuesday	Wednesday	Thursday	Friday	Saturday	Sunday
7 P.M.	Circle of Riches **8**	Friendly Neighbors **13**	Peril **59**	Twist City **18**	Relatives Rumble **4**	Toodles **22**	Judge Julie **68**
8 P.M.	Everybody Leaves Richard **3**	The Sullivans **14**	Hippy Daze **62**	Just Tell Me **43**	Who Wants to Be a Matador **51**	Shipwreck **73**	Doherty, Utah Baker **7**
9 P.M.	WWF—World Whispering Federation **89**	Charlie Tulip **9**	The Not Very Late Show **85**	Little Horse on the Prairie **29**	10/10 **1**	Cotton Puff Girls **56**	America's Most Washed **47**
10 P.M.	RSVP Yellow **97**	Danger! **41**	Fries to Order **2**	The West Park **54**	South Wing **16**	The Penny Poppy Show **21**	38 Minutes **38**
11 P.M.	News at Eleven **5**	America's Most Boring Home Videos **59**	Wednesday Night Prerecorded **61**	When Snowmen Attack **49**	Inside the Actor's Locker **31**	The Price Is High **6**	The Y-Factors **100**

YOUR TURN

Make a list all the prime numbers under 100 on the back of this page.

Date _____

Name _____

Exponents

Little Number, BIG Impact

A shortcut for writing 2 x 2 x 2 is 2^3. The number that is written above and to the right of another number is called an exponent. Insert an exponent to the right of each number in column A so that it equals the number in column B. We've done the first one for you.

	A	B
1.	4^2	16
2.	6☐	216
3.	8☐	64
4.	9☐	729
5.	2☐	68
6.	4☐	256
7.	3☐	2,187
8.	11☐	14,641
9.	25☐	15,625
10.	47☐	103,823

Tic-Tac-Decimal

One row in each grid below adds up to a number in one of the other boxes in the grid. The row can be across, down, or diagonal. Put a line through the row and circle the row's sum in each grid. We've done the first one for you.

1.

5.1	11.0	4.0
9.2	6.0	2.3
(15.2)	19.0	4.1

4.

12.3	43.4	16.7
13.4	15.1	14.9
41.5	8.6	36.8

2.

2.0	3.1	1.7
6.2	3.5	6.8
5.4	2.1	1.2

5.

20.9	11.7	30.6
3.5	55.9	8.2
5.0	5.4	17.1

3.

6.3	9.3	18.9
13.9	7.1	12.3
5.6	2.5	3.5

6.

10.2	9.7	.33
3.4	.29	.5
.46	2.1	1.08

Activities for Fast Finishers: Math Scholastic Professional Books

Date _____

Name _____

Math

Defying Physics

Remove one number from the middle or bottom row of each pyramid so that the remaining numbers will add up exactly to the number at the top of the pyramid. Don't worry, the pyramid will not fall! Circle the number you would remove for each. We've done the first one for you.

 TIP *Make sure the decimal points line up when you add. Round up to the nearest tenth if you have to.*

1.

	2.71		
.13	.21	.8	
.28	.6	.5	.19	.4

4.

	7.15		
5.2	.7	.32	
4.3	.34	.3	.75	.44

2.

	6.5		
.7	1.4	3.0	
.17	.6	.89	.22	.12

5.

	6.55		
.98	.38	.34	
.115	.27	1.30	.20	.30
.23	.432	.56	.01	1.1	1.23	.4

3.

	11.99		
6.1	2.0	.41	
.18	1.6	.2	1.35	.1

6.

	16.5		
.45	.675	1.4	
2.13	.33	.18	.02	4.1
.18	.09	1.3	.77	.945	3.2	.88

YOUR TURN

Make your own pyramid for a friend or family member to solve.

FAST FINISHERS

Date _____

Name _____

Puzzle Time

What's the power of a dot? A lot, if the dot is a decimal point! Complete the cross-number puzzle below by rounding each number as indicated. (Hint: Place each decimal point in a square of its own.) We've done the first one for you.

	Across		Down
1.	.347 to tenths	**2.**	36.7435 to hundredths
3.	635.127 to hundredths	**3.**	63.566 to tenths
5.	8.55 to tenths	**4.**	10.6589 to thousandths
7.	63.87 to tenths	**6.**	9.3573 to hundredths
10.	2.456 to tenths	**11.**	5.679 to tenths
12.	1, 768.677 to hundredths		

FAST FINISHERS

Math

Time for a Laugh

What did the judge give the thief who stole a calendar? To find the answer to this riddle, you need to subtract decimals. Solve each problem below. Then circle the letter next to the correct answer for each equation. Use the letters to find the riddle answer in the box below. We've done the first one for you.

TIP *Make sure you line up the decimal points!*

Judge

1. 3.74 − 2.54 =
  Ⓣ 1.2
  A 1.4

2. 5.1 − 2.72 =
  B 2.67
  L 2.38

3. 10.95 − 5.43
  E 5.52
  Z 5.89

4. 0.48 − 0.27
  I 0.29
  V 0.21

5. 8.8 − 4.4 =
  U 4.6
  W 4.4

6. 6.23 − 0.56 =
  Q 4.67
  O 5.67

7. 7 − 2.35
  B 3.54
  N 4.65

8. 5 − 0.6 =
  S 4.4
  I 4.35

9. 1 − 0.75 =
  T 0.25
  P 1.25

10. 72.6 − 18.9 =
  M 53.7
  R 65.3

11. 9 − 8.92
  F 0.32
  H 0.08

12. 21.45 − 0.92 =
  Y 20.55
  E 20.53

Riddle Answer											
T	__	__	__	__	__		__	__	__	__	__
1	5	3	2	4	12		10	6	7	9	11	8

Date _____

Name _____

Get Cracking!

There's a fraction that describes the break pattern in each set of broken objects below. Do the math and identify the fraction, making sure you reduce it to its lowest terms. We've done the first one for you.

Broken objects			Break pattern
1. light bulbs			
20-watt bulb broke into 10 pieces	60-watt bulb broke into 30 pieces	100-watt bulb broke into 50 pieces	Number of pieces = 1/2 wattage
2. ceramic vases			
15-pound vase broke into 3 pieces	30-pound vase broke into 6 pieces	105-pound vase broke into 21 pieces	
3. sheets of glass			
20-square-foot sheet of glass broke into 5 pieces	96-square-foot sheet of glass broke into 24 pieces	400-square-foot sheet of glass broke into 100 pieces	
4. dinner plates			
12-year-old plate broke into 4 pieces	30-year-old plate broke into 10 pieces	72-year-old plate broke into 24 pieces	
5. computer monitor			
16-inch monitor broke into 12 pieces	20-inch monitor broke into 15 pieces	24-inch monitor broke into 18 pieces	
6. crystal lamp			
10-inch-tall lamp broke into 6 pieces	15-inch-tall lamp broke into 9 pieces	20-inch-tall lamp broke into 12 pieces	
7. glass mirror			
48-inch round mirror broke into 42 pieces	32-inch round mirror broke into 28 pieces	72-inch round mirror broke into 63 pieces	
8. French doors			
15 window panes, 10 cracked	18 window panes, 12 cracked	21 window panes, 14 cracked	

FAST FINISHERS

Math

Balloon Journey

The helium-filled balloons listed below just landed in your yard. How many miles did they travel to get there? Do the math and find out. Then circle the color of the balloon that traveled the farthest. We've done the first one for you.

Color of balloon	Distance traveled	Total miles
1. red	traveled 440 miles over land plus $\frac{5}{8}$ as many miles over water	$440 \times \frac{5}{8} = 275$ $440 + 275 = 715$ miles
2. yellow	traveled 580 miles over water plus $\frac{3}{4}$ as many miles over land	
3. purple	traveled 234 miles over land plus $\frac{2}{3}$ as many miles over water	
4. green	traveled 702 miles over land plus $\frac{7}{9}$ as many miles over water	
5. orange	traveled 693 miles over water plus $\frac{6}{7}$ as many miles over land	
6. blue	traveled 714 miles over land plus $\frac{1}{6}$ as many miles over water	
7. white	traveled 820 miles over water plus $\frac{4}{5}$ as many miles over land	
8. black	traveled 368 miles over land plus $\frac{7}{8}$ as many miles over water	
9. pink	traveled 125 miles over land plus $\frac{2}{5}$ as many miles over water	
10. silver	traveled 600 miles over land plus $\frac{1}{6}$ as many miles over water	

Fast Finishers

Math

Date _____

Name _____

Fractions

Fraction Action

Only one fraction on the list, when multiplied by the whole numbers on the path, results in a whole number every time. To identify which fraction this is, multiply each fraction by each whole number on the path. Circle the fraction when you know which one is the right answer.

Example: $\frac{1}{3}$ x 24 = 8

Fraction list: $\frac{1}{4}$ $\frac{1}{6}$ $\frac{1}{3}$ $\frac{1}{8}$

Start →	24	72	108	144	216	648
						822
						852
1,512	1,500	1,392	1,296	1,200	1,050	924
1,776						
1,806						
1,920	2,028	2,061	2,343	2,586	3,435	4,356
						Finish

42

Activities for Fast Finishers: Math Scholastic Professional Books

Date _____

Name _____

Out of This World

Which planets have the longest years* in our solar system? The answers are on this page. But to figure them out you'll need to find the least common denominator (LCD) for each pair of fractions. Then find the letter for each LCD at the bottom of the page. Use these letters to write the names of each planet in the blanks.

* Period of orbit around Sun, in Earth years/days.

Example: to find the LCD for $\frac{1}{4}$ and $\frac{1}{5}$:

Find the first few multiples of each denominator.

    Multiples of 4: 4, 8, 12, 16, ⑳, 24

    Multiples of 5: 5, 10, 15, ⑳, 25

    LCD = 20

1. $\frac{4}{5} , \frac{4}{9}$ $\frac{1}{2} , \frac{5}{7}$ $\frac{2}{3} , \frac{9}{14}$ $\frac{5}{9} , \frac{5}{12}$ $\frac{4}{5} , \frac{5}{4}$

    LCD = _____ _____ _____ _____ _____

The planet with the longest year in our solar system (247 years, 256 days) is:

_____

2. $\frac{5}{16} , \frac{2}{3}$ $\frac{3}{8} , \frac{23}{28}$ $\frac{8}{9} , \frac{4}{15}$ $\frac{13}{18} , \frac{1}{4}$ $\frac{5}{42} , \frac{1}{1}$ $\frac{7}{12} , \frac{15}{16}$ $\frac{51}{56} , \frac{1}{1}$

    LCD = _____ _____ _____ _____ _____ _____ _____

The planet with the second longest year in our solar system (164 years, 298 days) is:

_____

3. $\frac{1}{10} , \frac{2}{5}$ $\frac{1}{6} , \frac{1}{4}$ $\frac{1}{36} , \frac{5}{6}$ $\frac{1}{42} , \frac{1}{1}$ $\frac{17}{30} , \frac{11}{20}$ $\frac{5}{48} , \frac{1}{1}$

    LCD = _____ _____ _____ _____ _____

The planet with the fourth longest year in our solar system (29 years, 168 days) is:

_____

S = 10	N = 48	P = 45	T = 36	R = 60	O = 20
U = 42	J = 28	I = 30	E = 56	L = 14	A = 12

Date _____

Name _____

Improper Ages

On Numerdenominaria, ages are measured in
improper fractions. To make the conversion to
Earth years, you'll have to change each fraction
to a mixed number. (Hint: Be sure it's in simplest
terms.) Then answer the questions below.

	Age on Numerdenominaria	Age on Earth
Algie	$\frac{44}{8}$	
Rusie	$\frac{31}{9}$	
Oma	$\frac{36}{10}$	
Newtie	$\frac{21}{6}$	
Lola	$\frac{120}{16}$	
Elbie	$\frac{144}{12}$	
Matia	$\frac{25}{10}$	
Hecta	$\frac{100}{22}$	
Octo	$\frac{63}{14}$	
Velo	$\frac{130}{20}$	

1. Who is the oldest Numerdenominaria citizen? _____

2. Who is the youngest? _____

3. How old will Algie be in two years? (Give your answer in Numerdenominaria
and Earth years.) _____

Date _____

Name _____

Everything Must Go!

The Velocity Vulture Appliance Store is having a big sale. Prices on all items are being reduced in an unusual way. Read the sale terms listed below and then calculate the new price of each item. If an item number is divisible by more than one number, choose the bigger percentage. We've done the first one for you.

25% off

Sale terms: Every item whose model number is evenly divisible by:

12 or 14, is on sale 25% off

13 or 15, is on sale 20% off

20 or 22, is on sale 30% off

27 or 29, is on sale 15% off

Item/model number	Price before sale	Evenly divisible by	Price after sale
1. Pro Chopper 880	$600	20 and 22 (on sale 30% off)	$420 ($600 x .30 = $180; $600 – 180 = $420)
2. Deluxe Dishwasher 1160	$500		
3. Golden Knight 896	$700		
4. Quickmaster 1200	$650		
5. Great Chef 720	$800		
6. Wash 'N Clean 1566	$480		
7. Dry 'N White 1400	$400		
8. Below Zero 962	$975		

Which item is least expensive after the discount? _____

Date _____

Name _____

Get With the Team

Below are resolutions being considered by the newly formed Team of Nations. In all, there are seven countries in attendance with a total of 38 delegates. For a resolution to pass, it must receive at least 66% of the vote. Imagine you are the voting inspector in charge of keeping track of the votes. For each resolution, figure out the total that voted yes and the percent that is of the total number of delegates. Then write whether or not it passed. We've done the first one for you.

Resolution	Yes votes	Percent that voted yes	Did it pass?
1. *Free ice cream for all citizens on Mondays.*	Zania 2 Funstan 2 Laughland 3 New Chuckles 4 South Giggle 1 **Total:** Smilinea 2 20 Jokesalot 6	To find percentage: $20 \div 38 = .52$ Answer: 52%	No
2. *Mandatory naps.*	Zania 0 Funstan 3 Laughland 1 New Chuckles 2 South Giggle 3 **Total:** Smilinea 5 ____ Jokesalot 3		
3. *A skate park in every town.*	Zania 1 Funstan 6 Laughland 2 New Chuckles 3 South Giggle 2 **Total:** Smilinea 8 ____ Jokesalot 7		
4. *Ban on lima beans.*	Zania 1 Funstan 5 Laughland 4 New Chuckles 1 South Giggle 2 **Total:** Smilinea 7 ____ Jokesalot 11		

Math

Date _____

Name _____

Percents

Dino Bone Zone

The Downtown Museum of Modern Antiquities and Normal Oddities has a strange collection of dinosaur bones. They have found species that no one else has. Some of their dinosaur skeletons, however, are incomplete. Use the information on the chart to rank these dinosaurs in order of most complete (1) to least complete (8) depending on how many bones are missing. We've done the first one for you.

Dinosaur	Number of bones present	Number of bones missing	Percentage of skeleton that is complete	Rank
1. Upstairosaurus	402	28	402 + 28 = 430 total bones 402 ÷ 430 = .93 .93 x 100 = 93% Answer: 93% complete	
2. Licorice Rex	249	231		
3. Digitalodor	10	8		
4. Fireworkadyl	185	260		
5. Bookmarkodon	56	399		
6. Studyoteratops	356	21		
7. Chaseoraptor	297	54		
8. Percentonychus	176	95		

Milk Money

The Early Bird Elementary School made a strange investment—a real cow! Now students can get milk at no charge (if the cow is in a good mood, that is!). The students below plan to take advantage of the milk money savings. Look at how much they spent each day on milk, what they want to buy, and the cost of that item. Set up an equation that will tell them how many days they'll have to save until they can afford the item next to their name. We've done the first one for you.

 It's okay if the equation isn't exactly the cost of the item they want to buy, it just has to be enough.

Student	Milk money per day	Item wants to buy	Cost	How many days until he/she can afford the item?
1. Sue	$0.25	book	$5.65	23 days $5.65 ÷ .25 = 22 R 15
2. Jacob	$0.80	jump rope	$10.95	
3. Louis	$0.35	clock radio	$17.50	
4. Molly	$0.40	magazine subscription	$20.00	
5. Ralph	$0.25	book bag	$26.47	
6. Rosita	$0.50	scooter	$59.99	
7. Tyrone	$0.75	hit CD	$15.75	
8. Karen	$0.30	winter jacket	$65.00	

Money Matters

The stores on the chart below have sold out of two products. If they could reorder only one of the two that they're missing at this time, which one should they choose? Do the math based on the sales information provided from each store. Tell which item each store should reorder and explain why.

Store	Product 1/ price	Product 1/ average daily sales	Product 2/ price	Product 2/ average daily sales	Which should they reorder?
1. Gretehen's General Store	dishwasher detergent/ $2.99	10	raisin flakes cereal/ $3.19	8	detergent (10 x 2.99 = $29.90; 8 x 3.19 = $25.52)
2. The Emporium	chocolate bar/$0.60	18	gum/ $0.49	21	
3. One-Stop Shop	apples/ $0.25	30	bananas/ $0.25	28	
4. Mr. Deals	pasta/ $1.09	12	soup/ $0.89	10	
5. Grocer Green	lettuce/ $1.00	26	cucumbers/ $0.69	30	
6. Stuff Mart	batteries/ $3.99	15	light bulbs/ $2.09	23	
7. Sports World	soccer shirts/ $15.75	7	running shoes/ $31.50	4	
8. Try & Buy	baby blue party dress/ $65.00	3	navy blue silk tie/ $27.00	7	

Date _____

Name _____

Find Your Way Out

It all started with Hansel and Gretel dropping bread crumbs on their path through the forest to find their way out. Since then, others have used various (natural or biodegradable) items instead of bread crumbs to do the same. If the forest explorers below drop *one item every 50 meters*, will they have enough to find their way out? You'll need to know the metric system to find out. Do the math, then write yes or no in the chart below.

 The explorers won't drop an item at the very start or at the very end of their path.

Forest explorer	What does he/she drop?	How many does he/she have?	How far will he/she walk?	Will he/she have enough?
1. Jesse	corn kernels	75	3 kilometers	
2. Warner	pine cones	30	2 km	
3. Mara	cotton balls	65	2.5 km	
4. Brianne	peanut shells	40	1 km	
5. Sylvia	big acorns	75	4 km	
6. Tomas	popcorn kernels	100	7 km	
7. Alex	daisies	25	1.25 km	
8. Jud	index cards	50	2.75 km	
9. Nathan	sunflower seeds	20	1.5 km	
10. Livia	shells	40	3.5 km	

Date _____

Name _____

Guess Your Best

The four math statements in each box below are missing an operation symbol (+ , − , x, ÷). Which one of the four math statements could NOT equal the number in the middle, no matter which of the four operations you try? Try out each possibility. Then circle the correct one and explain your reasoning in the space provided. There is only one correct answer for each. We've done the first one for you.

1.

6?2		1?3
	4	
1?5		1?4

The answer is **1?5**, because none of the four symbols (+, -, ÷, x) would make this equal four. Here is how the other three would equal four: 6 − 2, 1 + 3, 1 x 4.

4.

3?162		89?35
	54	
28?26		3?18

_____

_____

_____

2.

2?4		10?2
	8	
9?1		56?8

_____

_____

_____

5.

3?6		90?5
	18	
79?62		22?4

_____

_____

_____

3.

93?86		91?13
	7	
96?14		5?2

_____

_____

_____

6.

63?39		47?57
	4	
6?17		160?58

_____

_____

_____

Date _____

Name _____

Mark and Darcy's Game

Mark and Darcy made their own dartboard, then played a few games. Their dartboard was not designed like a typical board. For one thing, it was not round but rectangular! Here is what it looked like (the numbers inside each square indicate the points a spot is worth). Answer the questions below based on the information found on the dartboard. In some cases, there is more than one correct answer.

15	17	18	20	20	20	18	17	15
17	25	25	27	27	27	25	25	17
18	25	30	33	35	33	30	25	18
20	27	33	37	40	37	33	27	20
20	27	35	40	50 BULL'S EYE	40	35	27	20
20	27	33	37	20	37	33	27	20
18	25	30	33	35	33	30	25	18
17	25	25	27	27	27	25	25	17
15	17	18	20	20	20	18	17	15

1. Darcy landed on a 33 on her first toss. Mark tied her in 2 tosses. On what spots did he land?

_____

2. Mark got a bull's eye. Darcy tied him in 3 tosses. On what spots could she have landed?

_____

3. Darcy got a bull's eye. Mark tied her in 2 tosses. On what spots could he have landed?

_____

4. Darcy had 127 points. Could Mark beat her in 3 tosses, without a bull's eye?

_____

5. When Mark wasn't looking, Darcy claimed she got 95 points in 2 tosses. Was she tricking him?

_____

6. Mark had 81 points when Darcy tied him in 3 tosses. On what spots could she have landed?

_____

FAST FINISHERS

Math

On the Wall

Four cousins kept track of how much they grew for five years. Two cousins recorded their height in inches, and two cousins recorded it in feet. In order to compare, you'll have to do some math. The chart below tells you how each child grew over the years. Use it to answer the questions below.

Child	Height by year					
	2000	**2001**	**2002**	**2003**	**2004**	**2005**
Noah	4 ft 4 in	4 ft 6 in	4 ft 10 in	5 ft 3 in	5 ft 4 in	5 ft 5 in
Alison	51 in	54 in	56 in	56 in	59 in	62 in
Sandra	4 ft	4 ft 7 in	5 ft	5 ft 2 in	5 ft 3 in	5 ft 4 in
Nick	49 in	49 in	53 in	57 in	59 in	59 in

1. What years does this chart cover? _____

2. Who is tallest in each of these years?

   2001 _____   2002 _____   2004 _____

3. Who is shortest in each of these years?

   2000 _____   2003 _____   2005 _____

4. Who grew the most during the time span covered by the chart? _____

5. How much did the person in the previous question grow during these years? _____

6. Who grew the least during the time span covered by the chart? _____

7. How much did the person in the previous question grow during these years? _____

8. Who had the biggest growth spurt from one year to the next? Include the years and how much the person grew. _____

9. Which two kids didn't grow at all from one year to the next? During what years? _____

10. Predict who you think will end up being the tallest in the group based on the information from the chart. _____

Date _____

Name _____

Speed Readers

Ms. Gordon's class was asked to read *Adventures of the Time Travelers* in one week. They could read as much or little per day as they wanted, as long as they all finished on time. The chart below shows how some students divided their reading. Use it to answer the questions.

Student	Chapters read by Ms. Gordon's class						
	Mon.	**Tues.**	**Wed.**	**Thurs.**	**Fri.**	**Sat.**	**Sun.**
Alan	1–3	4	5–8	0	9–10	11–13	14–16
Lois	0	0	1	2	3–6	7–13	14–16
Barry	1–4	5	6	7–15	0	16	0
June	1–2	3–4	5–9	10–11	12–13	14–15	16
Grant	1–8	9	0	10–11	0	12	13–16
Scott	1–5	6–7	8–10	11–16	0	0	0

1. Based on information in this chart, how many chapters do students have to read over how many days? _____

2. Who was first to finish the book, and on what day did this happen? _____

3. Who read chapter 9 first, and on what day? _____

4. Who read the most chapters in one day, how many was it, and on what day did he or she do this? _____

5. What is the earliest day you could ask someone what chapter 7 is about, and whom would you ask? _____

6. Who was the last to read chapter 13, and on what day? _____

7. Who read the most on the weekend, and how many chapters? _____

8. Who was the second to finish the book, and on what day? _____

9. On what day were the least chapters read by the class? _____

10. On what day did the class read the most chapters? _____

Math

FAST FINISHERS

Think Inside the Box

How good are you at visualizing shapes? Answer the questions about each figure. It looks easy, but be careful! Keeping track of what lines belong to which boxes can be tricky. You can only count individual boxes with no lines inside! We've done the first one for you.

1.

    a. How many boxes can be made? ____four____

    b. How many boxes are already fully made? _____

    c. How many are exactly three-fourths made? _____

    d. How many are exactly half made? _____

    e. How many are exactly one-fourth made? _____

    f. How many are not begun? _____

2.

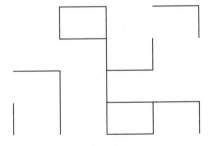

    a. How many boxes of the same size can be made? _____

    b. How many boxes are already fully made? _____

    c. How many are exactly three-fourths made? _____

    d. How many are exactly half made? _____

    e. How many are exactly one-fourth made? _____

    f. How many are not begun? _____

YOUR TURN

Using graph paper, create your own box of smaller boxes, but leave some lines out like the ones above. Ask a friend or family member to answer the same questions about your boxes as you just did.

In Search of Numbers

Numeria is a world where numbers are living beings, and they have all the same things humans on Earth do, such as cars, houses, and newspapers.

This is a page from the classified section of a Numeria newspaper. Read each listing and determine what other number each number is looking for.

NUMERIA TIMES CLASSIFIEDS

WANTED: Number between 1–5 but no odds and nothing evenly divisible by 4

1. _____

LOOKING: Two-digit number with no straight lines, and no 0s, 3s, or 9s; larger number first

4. _____

SEARCHING FOR: Largest two-digit number that can be multiplied by 3 and still be less than 40

2. _____

ARE YOU THE ONE? Largest three-digit number less than 566 whose digits get consecutively higher

5. _____

HELP ME FIND: Largest two-digit number whose digits equal 11 when added together; no 2s or 3s

3. _____

WHERE IS: Only number between 100–116 that is evenly divisible by 2, 4, 6, and 9

6. _____

YOUR TURN

Write a classified ad in search of the number 8.

Alien Phenomenon

The year is 3002. Scientists have just discovered another galaxy with a solar system in which all nine of its planets are home to strange robots. There are even robots on the asteroids in the asteroid belt between the fourth and fifth planets.

Scientists notice a strange phenomenon. In this newly discovered galaxy, robots on planets inside the asteroid belt have *four* fingers per hand. Robots outside the asteroid belt have *five* fingers per hand. But, they don't all have only two hands like we do! Below is a list of planets in the new galaxy. Write whether each planet is inside or outside the asteroid belt using all the clues. We've done the first one for you.

Planet	Total number of fingers its robots have	Total number of hands	Inside or outside the asteroid belt
1. Traeh	10	2	outside
2. Sunev	12		
3. Rucremy	16		
4. Smar	35		
5. Retipuj	25		
6. Rutans	4		
7. Sunaru	8		
8. Enutpen	30		
9. Otulp	28		

Why? Write equations that show why your answers are correct.

1. __10 ÷ 5 = 2__

2. _____

3. _____

4. _____

5. _____

6. _____

7. _____

8. _____

9. _____

One-Hit Wonder

The Hamburger Sisters had one number-one hit in their rock-and-roll career, but they can't remember which year it happened! Eight possible years are listed in the box below. Use the clues to eliminate all but the correct year. (Hint: Not every clue eliminates a year.)

Possible years			
1983	1986	1989	1992
1984	1988	1990	1995

Clues	Year(s) eliminated
1. No hits were on the chart between 1991 and 1993.	
2. The band formed in 1984.	
3. The only year in which the band took a vacation was 1989.	
4. The band had no top-ten hits in its first three years.	
5. The band never had a hit on both the U.S. and British charts at the same time.	
6. Every song they released in 1987 and 1988 went only as high as number 3.	
7. None of the band's songs were released after 1994.	
8. The band broke up in 1995.	
9. The band's most popular single in 1990 was on the British chart.	

The Hamburger Sisters' number-one hit was in the year _____.

Date _____

Name _____

Break the Code!

On the planet Rebmun, numbers don't have the same meaning as on ours. In the equations below, *only the answer* has been translated into the correct equivalent you would find on Earth. Your job is to translate the rest. Based on each equation's sum, figure out what each Rebmun number is worth on Earth and fill out the code chart on the bottom of the page. Use the blanks to help you keep track of your work. You don't have to solve the problems in order; in fact, it is probably easier to skip around! We've done the first one for you.

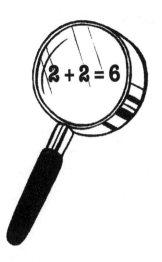

1. 2 + 2 = 6   (2 in Rebmun equals 3 on Earth, because 3 + 3 = 6) _____

2. 3 + 7 = 9 _____

3. 9 + 9 = 8 _____

4. 4 + 1 = 7 _____

5. 7 + 7 = 0 _____

6. 9 + 2 = 7 _____

7. 0 + 6 = 7 _____

8. 5 + 4 = 9 _____

9. 6 + 7 = 2 _____

10. 5 + 5 =16 _____

The Code (Rebmun number = Earth number) is as follows:

0 =	1 =	2 = 3	3 =	4 =	5 =	6 =	7 =	8 =	9 =

Date _____

Name _____

Oops, Wrong Number

Below is a list of wrong numbers. For each wrong number, use the clue to determine the number the caller meant to dial.

Wrong number	Clue for correct number	Correct number
1. 914-4258	completely reverse the order	
2. 451-1362	reverse the two sets of numbers whose sum is 9	
3. 654-6922	change every even number to its half	
4. 288-2537	replace odd numbers with the next highest even number	
5. 486-2427	change any number that can be evenly divided in half to a 6	
6. 250-7337	triple every number less than 4	
7. 529-7395	rewrite the numbers in ascending order	
8. 815-6224	subtract the last number from the first number and change any numbers evenly divisible by 2 to product of 2 x 2	
9. 273-1561	reverse the two numbers whose product is 30 and reverse the two numbers whose product is 14	
10. 455-6859	replace certain numbers so you'll end up with a number pattern of plus one, minus two	

YOUR TURN

Make up a phone number as the wrong number, and create a clue for a friend or family member to determine the correct number.

Activities for Fast Finishers: Math Scholastic Professional Books

Answers

PAGE 6: *Time for the Future*
1. 1866
2. 1969
3. 1990
4. 1947
5. 1901
6. 1899

PAGE 7: *Many Pennies Lane*
2. "700 Pennies Lane"
3. "1,525 Pennies Lane"
4. "555 Pennies Lane"
5. "219 Pennies Lane"
6. "4,000 Pennies Lane"
7. "8,101 Pennies Lane"
8. "199 Pennies Lane"
9. "101 Pennies Lane"
10. "4,550 Pennies Lane"
11. "400 Pennies Lane"
12. "100,000 Pennies Lane"

PAGE 8: *Half Time*
2. 15 + 7 + 12 + ⟨34⟩ = 68
3. ⟨11⟩ + 3 + 6 + 2 = 22
4. 21 + 38 + ⟨67⟩ + 8 = 134
5. 61 + ⟨94⟩ + 33 = 188
6. 24 + 30 + 100 + ⟨180⟩ + 26 = 360
7. 77 + ⟨368⟩ + 46 + 245 = 736
8. ⟨610⟩ + 401 + 102 + 107 = 1,220
9. 239 + 812 + ⟨1,329⟩ + 278 = 2,658
10. 1,035 + 1,507 + ⟨5,421⟩ + 2,879 = 10,842

Your Turn: In each equation remove the largest number, which is always half of the original sum.

PAGE 9: *Grab, Add 'N Win*
1. Deena—$80.00
2. Noelle—$100.50
3. Gerry—$101.88
4. Raphael—$100.25
5. Francesca—$101.31
6. ⟨Joel—$101.28⟩
7. Alexandra—$89.74
8. Samantha—$122.74
9. Sebastian—$101.48
10. Anthony—$64.99

PAGE 10: *Desperately Seeking 68*
2. 797 → 77 − 9 = 68
3. 9532 → 93 − 25 = 68
4. 31013 → 101 − 33 = 68
5. 66831 → 36 − 68 = 68
6. 21058 → 50 − 42 = 68
7. 012017 → 170 − 102 = 68
8. 972353 → 395 − 327 = 68
9. 123559 → 591 − 523 = 68
10. 679679 → 767 − 699 = 68

PAGE 11: *Numberless Subtraction*
2. quintuplets – quartet = **1** (quintuplets are 5 siblings, quartet is a group of 4)
3. Valentine's Day – Groundhog Day = **12** (Valentine's is February 14, Groundhog February 2; other reasonable answers, 214 – 22 = 192.)
4. octagon – pentagon = **3** (octagon has 8 sides, pentagon has 5)
5. planets in our solar system – continents = **2** (9 planets, 7 continents)
6. U.S. senators – U.S. states = **50** (100 Senators, 50 states)
7. minutes in an hour – days in September = **30** (hour has 60 minutes, September has 30 days)
8. Declaration of Independence – Columbus lands in the Americas = **284** (1776, 1492)
9. millennium year – The year exactly one century before the millennium = **100** (2000 – 1900). (Some people consider the millennium year 2001, so 101 is also acceptable.)
10. tetrahedron – quadrant = **0** (4 – 4; *tetra-* and *quad-* are both prefixes that mean four.)

PAGE 12: *Big Spenders*
1. Juan—$6.02, 4
2. Kevin—$11.41, 1
3. Mike—$1.86, 7
4. Dara—$4.27, 6
5. Randi—$10.14, 3
6. Seth—$4.81, 5
7. Darren—$10.72, 2
8. Raquel—$.77, 8

PAGE 13: *A Perfect Match*
Numbers in column 2 are rearranged so that they're next to their 343 partner.

Column 1	Column 2
656	999
251	594
854	511
799	456
686	343
475	818
976	633
466	123
1,257	914
883	1,226

PAGE 14: *Eight Is Great*
Explanation: Stephanie is eight in 2000, so she was born in 1992. Stephanie's father wears a badge reading "29," which means he was born 29 years before she was. 1992 – 29 = 1963, the year Stephanie's father was born. 1963 + 8 = 1971, the year Stephanie's father turned eight

1. father: 1963, 1971
2. mother: 1964, 1972
3. great-grandfather: 1913, 1921
4. great-grandmother: 1915, 1945
5. grandmother: 1937, 1923
6. grandfather: 1938, 1946
7. aunt: 1969, 1977
8. uncle: 1965, 1973
9. brother: 1987, 1995
10. dog: 1991, 1999
11. Answers will vary.

PAGE 15: *Radio Riches*
Amount of money per day (some dollar amounts are rounded up):
2. WSMK = $500.00
3. WMLC = $166.67
4. WAJD = $357.14
5. WMRP = $71.43
6. WWFD = $400.00
7. WPET = $250.00
8. WWHY = $333.33
9. WHIP = $600
10. ⟨WZZZ = $1,071⟩

PAGE 16: *Tag Sale Tally*

Purchases	Cost per CD	Rank (1= earliest, 10 = most recent)
12 CDs for $6.00	$0.50	2
8 CDs for $6.00	$0.75	3
4 CDs for $8.00	$2.00	8
7 CDs for $7.00	$1.00	5
9 CDs for $2.25	$0.25	1
4 CDs for $6.00	$1.50	6
5 CDs for $9.95	$1.99	7
4 CDs for $10.00	$2.50	9
5 CDs for $14.95	$2.99	10
5 CDs for $4.95	$0.99	4

PAGE 17: *Good Things Come in Threes*
2. 4 + 3 = 7, 7 − 4 = 3, 7 − 3 = 4, 3 + 4 = 7
3. 38 ÷ 2 = 19, 38 ÷ 19 = 2, 19 x 2 = 38, 2 x 19 = 38
4. 36 ÷ 9 = 4, 36 ÷ 4 = 9, 4 x 9 = 36, 9 x 4 = 36
5. 5 + 12 = 17, 12 + 5 = 17, 17 − 5 = 12, 17 − 12 = 5
6. 18 + 32 = 50, 32 + 18 = 50, 50 - 32 = 18, 50 - 32 = 18
7. 54 ÷ 9 = 6, 54 ÷ 6 = 9, 9 x 6 = 54, 6 x 9 = 54
8. 76 ÷ 19 = 4, 76 ÷ 4 = 19, 19 x 4 = 76, 4 x 19 = 76
9. 20 + 5 = 25, 5 + 20 = 25, 25 - 5 = 20, 25 - 20 = 5
10. 42 ÷ 7 = 6, 42 ÷ 6 = 7, 7 x 6 = 42, 6 x 7 = 42

Answers

PAGE 18: *Number Pole*

2. 12, ÷
3. 38, −
4. 64, x
5. 256, x
6. 166, +
7. 378, −
8. 480, ÷
9. 29, ÷

PAGE 19: *Meanie Genie*

Jake and **Daniela** should be circled *yes* because all their answers were correct! Cecilia is no, because she got the third equation wrong. 30 − 10 ÷ 2 = 25 (not 10).

PAGE 20: *Get the Scoop!*

1. Zaura—7 scoops
2. Ellis—18 scoops
3. Clara—18 scoops
4. Darby—15 scoops
5. Chang—7 scoops
6. Thelma—26 scoops
7. Deon—14 scoops
8. Gabriela—44 scoops
Gabriela is the new champion!

PAGE 21: *The Number Shuffle*

2. 390 + **876** = **1,266**
3. 486 + **1,266** = **1,752**
4. **1,752** − 654 = **1,098**
5. **1,098** x 3 = **3,294**
6. 6,402 − **3,294** = **3,108**
7. 59 + **150** = 209
8. 150 − 79 = **71**
9. 639 + **71** = **710**
10. **710** − 560 = **150**
11. **150** ÷ 30 = **5**
12. 85 − **5** = **80**

PAGE 22: *A-Maze-ing!*

START					
18 + 0	54 ÷ 3	32 ÷	36 +	48 ÷	98 ÷
42 ÷	9 x 2	20 +	12 x	54 +	9 −
19÷	4 + 14	19 +	15 −	4 x	22 ÷
25 +	108 ÷ 6	21 − 3	38 ÷	16 −	96 ÷
15 −	0 x	18 − 0	36 ÷ 2	36 − 18	100 +
3 −	26 ÷	78 ÷	8 x	2 x 9	14 x
7 x	28 +	24 ÷	56 ÷	199 − 181	17 −
64 ÷	92 ÷	12 −	44 ÷	18 x 1	702 ÷ 39
10 x	36 x	30 +	11 x	146 ÷	3 x 6
					FINISH

PAGE 23: *Lights, Camera, Action!*

1. 100   101   ⟨102⟩   106
2. 63   ⟨36⟩   26   16
3. 129   188   208   ⟨192⟩
4. ⟨5⟩   6   18   4
5. 80   ⟨82⟩   83   85
6. 199   145   ⟨198⟩   186
7. 80   ⟨82⟩   83   85

8. ⟨294⟩   298   268   283
9. 5,243   5,657   ⟨5,776⟩   6,557
10. 1,772   ⟨1,773⟩   1,779   1,777
11. 3,333   3,395   ⟨3,325⟩   3,345
12. 116   118   113   ⟨114⟩
Your Turn 53

PAGE 24: *Reaching the Top*

1. 586 ÷ 8 does not equal 86
2. 1,644 ÷ 68 does not equal 34
3. 259 ÷ 3 does not equal 65
4. 64 − 48 does not equal 15
José climbed the highest.

PAGE 25: *Harvest Riddle*

1. 64,8 (addition 72, subtraction 56, multiplication 512, division 8)
2. 18,3 (addition 21, subtraction 15, multiplication 54, division 6)
3. 35,7 (addition 42, subtraction 28, multiplication 245, division 5)
4. 6,0 (addition 6, subtraction 6, multiplication 0, division 0)

60	9	258	130	1
12	56	15	512	182
19	54	79	6	14
25	5	28	72	76
168	8	44	245	954
201	42	0	21	26
55	87	4	34	51

A harvestman, otherwise known as a daddy longlegs, is an arachnid that has 8 legs.

PAGE 26: *Three's a Charm*

	Evenly spaced trio	How many apart from one another?
2.	29, 36, 43	7
3.	18, 34, 50	16
4.	11, 46, 81	35
5.	63, 142, 221	79
6.	37, 58, 79	21
7.	13, 64, 115	51
8.	2,218; 2,323; 2,428	105

PAGE 27: *Find the Bookend*

	Which number belongs?	Beginning or end?	Description of pattern
2.	0	beginning	increases by 5
3.	3	beginning	increases by 5
4.	36	end	increases by 2, then 6, then 2, then 6, and so on
5.	27	end	decreases by 4
6.	123	beginning	decreases by 7
7.	7	end	+2, −1
8.	105	end	decreases by 1, increases by 8
9.	33	beginning	number added increases by one each time
10.	50	end	numbers decrease by half

PAGE 28: *Abracadabra!*

Group 1: All numbers have the exact same digits (in different orders), except these: 625 (Set A); 3,441 (Set B); 4,596 (Set C); 28,076 (Set D)
Group 2: All numbers are in reverse order, except these: 89 (Set A); 954 (Set B); 2,310 (Set C); 56,432 (Set D)
Group 3: The third digit is twice the first digit, except these: 170 (Set A); 781 (Set B); 172 (Set C); 201 (Set D)

PAGE 29: *Pyramid Challenge*

1. increases by 5 (missing numbers: 34, 54, 79)
2. increases by 7, then 2, then repeats (missing numbers: 0, 34, 45, 70)
3. decreases by 3 (missing numbers: 85, 70, 61, 55, 49)
4. decreases by 1, increases by 6, then repeats (missing numbers: 36, 46, 56, 61, 65)

Your Turn Pattern is ÷ 4, x 8, ÷ 4, x 8, etc. (missing numbers: 96, 48, 768, 384)

PAGE 30: *Think Ahead*

	A	B
2.	88	89
3.	222	234
4.	444	456
5.	77	789
6.	1,111	1,234
7.	3,333	2,345
8.	6,666	6,789
9.	8,888	8,910
10.	11,111	12,345

PAGE 31: *Hit the Road*

2. ⟨1⟩ 2 7 = 27 ÷ 9 = 3
3. ⟨2⟩ 6 3 = 63 ÷ 9 = 7
4. 1, 3 ⟨9⟩ 5 = 135 ÷ 9 = 15
5. 1, ⟨8⟩ 8 0 = 180 ÷ 9 = 20
6. 3, ⟨2⟩ 0 6 = 306 ÷ 9 = 34
7. 5, ⟨3⟩ 8 5 = 585 ÷ 9 = 65
8. 2 ⟨0⟩, 1 5 1 = 2,151 ÷ 9 = 239
9. 2 8, 5 3 ⟨1⟩ = 2,853 ÷ 9 = 317
10. ⟨9⟩ 4, 1 2 2 = 4,122 ÷ 9 = 458

Your Turn All the digits in a number evenly divisible by 9 (or a multiple of 9), add up to 9 (or a multiple of 9. E.g., 2,151 ÷ 9 = 239 and 2 + 1 + 5 + 1 = 9

PAGE 32: *Sum Good Facts*

1. 4 + 8 = 12
2. 12 + 36 = 48
3. 27 + 32 = 59
4. 63 + 27 = 90
5. 45 + 72 = 117, in 1931
6. 12 + 48 + 90 = 150

Answers

PAGE 33: *STRENGTH in Numbers*

1=A	6=F	11=K	16=P	21=U	26=Z
2=B	7=G	12=L1	17=Q	22=V	
3=C	8=H	3=M	18=R	23=W	
4=D	9=I	14=N	19=S	24=X	
5=E	10=J	15=O	20=T	25=Y	

2. 14 + 9 + 14 + 5 > 19 + 5+ 22 + 5 + 14
(42 > 65?) false

3. 20 + 23 + 15 > 15 + 14 + 5 (58 > 34?)
true

4. 20 + 23 + 5 + 12 + 22 + 5 > 5 + 9 + 7
+ 8 + 20 (87 > 49?) true

5. 5 + 9 + 7 + 8 + 20 + 25 > 19 + 9 + 24
+ 20 + 25 (74 > 97?) false

6. 6 + 9 + 6 + 20 + 25 > 20 + 8 + 9 + 18
+ 20 + 5 + 5 + 14 (66 > 99?) false

7. 20 + 8 + 9 + 18 + 20 + 25 + 15 + 14 +
5 > 20 + 23 + 5 + 14 + 20 + 25 + 15 +
14 + 5 (134 >141?) false

8. 19 + 5 + 22 + 5 + 14 + 20 + 25 + 6 +
15 + 21 + 18 > 6 + 15 + 18 + 20 + 25 +
19 + 5 + 22 + 5 + 14 (170 > 149?) true

PAGE 34: *Prime Time for Prime Numbers*

8 P.M.: Everybody Leaves Richard **3**;
Just Tell Me **43**; Shipwreck **73**;
Doherty, Utah Baker **7**

9 P.M.: WWF—World Whispering
Federation **89**; Little Horse on the Prairie **29**;
America's Most Washed **47**

10 P.M.: RSVP Yellow **97**; Danger **41**;
Fries to Order **2**

Your Turn 2, 3, 5, 7, 11, 13, 17, 19, 23,
29, 31, 37, 41, 43, 47, 53, 59, 61, 67, 71,
73, 79, 83, 89, 97

PAGE 35: *Little Number, BIG Impact*

2. 6^3 **7.** 3^7

3. 8^2 **8.** 11^4

4. 9^3 **9.** 25^3

5. 2^6 **10.** 47^3

6. 4^5

PAGE 36: *Tic-Tac-Decimal*

2.

2.0	3.1	1.7
6.2	3.5	(6.8)
5.4	2.1	1.2

5.

20.9	11.7	30.6
3.5	(55.9)	8.2
5.0	5.4	17.1

3.

6.3	9.3	(18.9)
13.9	7.1	12.3
5.6	2.5	3.5

6.

10.2	9.7	.33
3.4	.29	.5
.46	2.1	(1.08)

4.

12.3	(43.4)	16.7
13.4	15.1	14.9
41.5	8.6	36.8

PAGE 37: *Defying Physics*

2.

4.

3.

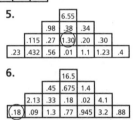

5.

6.

PAGE 38: *Puzzle Time*

PAGE 39: *Time for a Laugh*

2. (L) 2.38   **6.** (O) 5.67   **10.** (M) 53.7

3. (E) 5.52   **7.** (N) 4.65   **11.** (H) 0.08

4. (V) 0.21   **8.** (S) 4.4   **12.** (E) 20.53

5. (W) 4.4   **9.** (T) 0.25

Riddle Answer:

T W E L V E   M O N T H S
1 5 3 2 4 12   10 6 7 9 11 8

PAGE 40: *Get Cracking!*

Number of pieces =

2. $\frac{1}{5}$ weight

3. $\frac{1}{4}$ of square footage

4. $\frac{1}{3}$ age

5. $\frac{3}{4}$ size of monitor in inches

6. $\frac{3}{5}$ of height

7. $\frac{7}{8}$ of size

8. $\frac{2}{3}$ number of panes overall

PAGE 41: *Balloon Journey*

2. yellow traveled 580 + 435 = 1,015 miles

3. purple traveled 234 + 156 = 390 miles

4. green traveled 702 + 546 = 1,248 miles

5. orange traveled 693 + 594 = 1,287 miles

6. blue traveled 714 + 119 = 833 miles

7. white traveled the farthest: 820 +
656 = 1,476 miles

8. black traveled 368 + 322 = 690 miles

9. pink traveled 125 + 50 = 175 miles

10. silver traveled 600 + 100 = 700 miles

PAGE 42: *Fraction Action*

The answer is $\frac{1}{3}$.

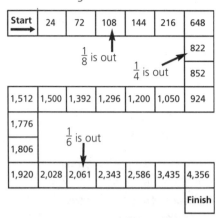

PAGE 43: *Out of This World*

1. LCD = 45, 14, 42, 36, 20; PLUTO

2. LCD = 48, 56, 45, 36, 42, 48, 56;
NEPTUNE

3. LCD = 10, 12, 36, 42, 60, 48; SATURN

PAGE 44: *Improper Ages*

Algie—5 $\frac{1}{2}$ Elbie—12

Rusie—3 $\frac{4}{9}$ Matia—2 $\frac{1}{2}$

Oma—3 $\frac{3}{5}$ Hecta—4 $\frac{6}{11}$

Newtie—3 $\frac{1}{2}$ Octo—4 $\frac{1}{2}$

Lola—7 $\frac{1}{2}$ Velo—6 $\frac{1}{2}$

The oldest citizen is Elbie who is 12.

The youngest is Matia who is 2 $\frac{1}{2}$.

In two years Algie will be $\frac{15}{2}$
on Numerdenominaria and 7 $\frac{1}{2}$ on Earth.

PAGE 45: *Everything Must Go!*

	Evenly divisible by	Price after sale
2.	22, 29	$350
3.	14	$525
4.	12, 15, 20	$520
5.	12, 15, 20	$560
6.	27	$408
7.	20	$310
8.	13	$780

Dry 'N White 1400

PAGE 46: *Get With the Team*

	Total votes	Percentage that voted yes	Did it pass?
2.	17	45%.	No
3.	29	76%	Yes
4.	31	82%	Yes

Answers

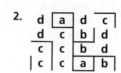

PAGE 47: *Dino Bone Zone*
Percentage of skeleton that is complete

2. 249/480 bones = 52% complete   6
3. 10/18 bones = 55% complete   5
4. 185/445 bones = 42% complete   7
5. 56/455 bones = 12% complete   8
6. 356/377 bones = 94% complete   1
7. 297/351 = 85% complete   3
8. 176/271 = 65% complete   4

PAGE 48: *Milk Money*

2. Jacob—14 days ($10.95 ÷ .80)
3. Louis—50 days ($17.50 ÷ .35)
4. Molly—50 days ($20.00 ÷ .40)
5. Ralph—106 days ($26.47 ÷ .25)
6. Rosita—120 days ($59.99 ÷ .50)
7. Tyrone—21 days ($15.75 ÷.75)
8. Karen—217 days ($65.00 ÷ .30)

PAGE 49: *Money Matters*

2. chocolate ($10.80) more than gum ($10.29)
3. apples ($7.50) more than bananas ($7.00)
4. pasta ($13.08) more than soup ($8.90)
5. lettuce ($26.00) more than cucumbers ($20.70)
6. batteries ($59.85) more than bulbs ($48.07)
7. running shoes ($126.00) is more than shirts ($110.25)
8. party dresses ($195.00) is more than ties ($189.00)

PAGE 50: *Find Your Way Out*

One kilometer is 1,000 meters, which is a little less than a mile (.62 of a mile, to be exact.) The total number of meters walked must be divided by 50, because the explorers will drop one item every 50 meters.

1. Jesse—yes; 3 km = 3,000 meters
   3,000 ÷ 50 = 60 items needed
2. Warner—no; 2 km = 2,000 meters
   2,000 ÷ 50 = 40 items needed
3. Mara—yes; 2.5 km = 2,500 meters
   2,500 ÷ 50 = 50 items needed
4. Brianne—yes; 1,000 meters
   1,000 ÷ 50 = 20 items needed
5. Sylvia—no; 4 km = 4,000 meters
   4,000 ÷ 50 = 80 items needed
6. Tomas—no; 7 km = 7,000 meters
   7,000 ÷ 50 = 140 items needed
7. Alex—yes; 1.25 km = 1,250 meters
   1,250 ÷ 50 = 25 items needed
8. Jud—no; 2.75 = 2,750 meters
   2,750 ÷ 50 = 55 items needed
9. Nathan—no; 1.5 km = 1,500 ÷ 50 = 30 items needed
10. Livia—no; 3.5 km = 3,500 ÷ 50 = 70 items needed

PAGE 51: *Guess Your Best*

2. 56?8
3. 96?14
4. 3?162
5. 79?62
6. 47?57

PAGE 52: *Mark and Darcy's Game*

1. 15, 18
2. 15, 17, 18 or 20, 15, 15
3. 25 twice; or 20, 30; or 15, 35
4. no, the highest he could get in 3 tosses with no bull's eye is 120
5. yes, because no two numbers on this board could add up to 95
6. 17, 27, 37 or 33, 33, 15

PAGE 53: *On the Wall*

1. five years from 2000–2005
2. 2001: Sandra; 2002: Sandra; 2004: Noah
3. 2000: Sandra; 2003: Alison; 2005: Nick
4. Sandra
5. ten inches
6. Nick
7. eight inches
8. Sandra grew seven inches from 2000 to 2001.
9. Nick and Alison. Nick didn't grow from 2000 to 2001 or from 2004 to 2005. Alison didn't grow from 2002 to 2003.
10. Sandra because she grew the most, 16 inches, in five years.

PAGE 54: *Speed Readers*

1. 16 chapters over 7 days
2. Scott, Thursday
3. Grant, Tuesday
4. Barry, 9, Thursday
5. Monday, Grant
6. Grant, Sunday
7. Lois, 10
8. Barry, Saturday
9. Tuesday, 7
10. Monday, 22

PAGE 55: *Think Inside the Box*

Key: full = a, three-fourths = b, half = c, one-fourth = d, not begun = e

1.

e	b
b	a

b. one
c. two
d. none (to be half made, exactly two of the four lines of the box must be there)
e. none
f. one

2.

d	a	d	c
d	c	b	d
c	c	b	d
c	c	a	b

a. sixteen
b. two
c. three
d. six
e. five
f. None

PAGE 56: *In Search of Numbers*

1. 2
2. 13
3. 74
4. 86
5. 456
6. 108

PAGE 57: *Alien Phenomenon*

	Total number of hands	Inside or outside the asteroid belt
2. Sunev	3	inside
3. Rucremy	4	inside
4. Smar	7	outside
5. Retipuj	5	outside
6. Rutans	1	inside
7. Sunaru	2	inside
8. Enutpen	6	outside
9. Otulp	7	inside

PAGE 58: *One-Hit Wonder*

1. 1992
2. 1983
3. none
4. 1984, 1986
5. none
6. 1988
7. 1995
8. none
9. 1990

Answer: 1989

PAGE 59: *Break the Code!*

The code (Rebmun number = Earth number):

0 = **5**	2 = **3**	4 = **1**	6 = **2**	8 = **7**
1 = **6**	3 = **9**	5 = **8**	7 = **0**	9 = **4**

2. 9 + 0 = 9
3. 4 + 4 = 8
4. 1 + 6 = 7
5. 0 + 0 = 0
6. 4 + 3 = 7
7. 5 + 2 = 7
8. 8 + 1 = 9
9. 2 + 0 = 2
10. 8 + 8 = 16

PAGE 60: *Oops, Wrong Number*

1. 852-4419
2. 541-1632
3. 352-3911
4. 288-2648
5. 666-6667
6. 650-7997
7. 235-5799
8. 415-4444
9. 723-1651
10. 453-4231